I CREATED MONEY TODAY BY DAVID GOMADZA

www.createbitcoin.world

www.twofuture.world

I CREATED MONEY TODAY BY DAVID GOMADZA

Copyright © 2024 David Gomadza

All rights reserved.

PAPERBACK ISBN: 9798343061291

I CREATED MONEY TODAY BY DAVID GOMADZA

DEDICATION

To money

CONTENTS

I CREATED MONEY TODAY BY DAVID GOMADZA

ACKNOWLEDGMENTS

I CREATED MONEY TODAY BY DAVID GOMADZA

paperbackisnb9798343061291

createbitcoin create a point of payment system in create code use atau only free allowed

i can then ask later

i ask but then where were you createbitcoin in hidding

18 lines

askwhybuthowsaypaywith createbitcoin

askwhatcanbebutisnotandwhyeverythingcanbebutmoneyisonlycreatebitcoin

askwhathasbeenbutcantbemoneyhasbeenbutcantbecreatebitcoinbutjustapaymentsystem

ifnotmoneythenwhatjustbitcoinjustcreatebitcoin

ifnotmoneythenwhatcouldthisbeitsbitcoinandcreatebitcoin

ifnotnowthenwhennoitsnownoworelseourcreatebitcoinwillsufferun necessarily

ifnotcreatebitcointhenwhatitsonlycreatebitcoin

ewhatcanbecreatebitcoinwithoutmoneyapaymentsystemonly

whatwasthatcanstillbebitcoinandnowcreatebitcoin

ifnotcreatebitcointhenwhatonlybitcoinandcreatebitcoin

whatcanbebutisnotmoneycantbebutcanbecreatebitcoin

whathasbeenbutisstillbebitcoinisstillbebutcanstillbesoascreatebitcoin

I CREATED MONEY TODAY BY DAVID GOMADZA

whatcanbedonetoincreasebitcoinvaluehencecreatebitcoineverythingthatpumpsanassetinsuchawaythatincreasevalue

whatistobebutcantbemoneycantbecreatebitcoinbutbothcanbemoney

whathasbeenbutcastillbebitcoinisandwillbesoascreatebitcoin

whatwillbebutcannolongerbejustnickel

whatcanbemoneybutcancomebacktolifejustnickel

ifmoneyisnickelthenwhatcanbeanickelpaymentsystemthesameascreatebitcoinandnickel

askwhatcanbebitcoincreatebitcoinandnickelinthefuturedavidgomadzaplanstorevivethenickelcurrencyhencenickelcanstillbecurrencyinthefuture

askifwearetoaddcreatebitcoinnickelandbitcointocurrencyasmoneythenwhatcanthisbethisisthefutureasin2026all3currencydominatetheuniversebutbitcoindiesleavingonlycreatebitcoinandnickelafterthegreatestescapeinthehistoryofmankindbybillgateswhosaidicanbutthenleftearthtojupiter

sellataucreatebitcoin789780forservicesrendered.start todaybitratevalueisUS$867890284x789780=US$282627292821232984

ifweasknowwhatcanbecreatebitcoinpricetomorrowthethisistheansweritwillbeUS$78989028467890

ifweaskwhatcanbethehighestbitrateeverandwhenforhimitsUS$28986789028767890284in2030becausehemasteredeverythingneededfirstonhisownandnowdiscoveraftersomewhichiscrucialsohisbitratejumpshighwhenhefindsoutthatiswhatisneeded

caniswapcreatebitcoinwithbitcoinandwhereyesaskbillgatestransfercodeandsendhimUS$387890284increatebitcoinasrequestedbymanuals

sendcreatebitcoinworthUS$387890284.start(billgatesaskfortransfercode)

whatistransfercode(892876387890286789 0285)acceptcancelhowcanireturnit?meaninghehasnowayofsendingitbutsayatauyoucanreturn tosender(everything)

twopointofpaymentsystemthatmatchescurrentbutisownedbytwo(tomorrowsworldorder)thatmeansthatwejustneedtoadd8linesonequationsabove(2lines)

askwhatcanbecreatebitcoinbackedbytwothisisthefutureasthingswillbe

askifwearetogeteverythingthenwhathatwillbewhatisneededbecauseallwillbepossibleatauhiddenforexpressclientsandpointofsystemforothers

askwhatcanbedonetocreatebitcoinforpointofsalepurchasesthencreate8reservesofhighestvaluefirst789890x8created

askwhatcanbeoftheseaccountsthennamethemasasertasatasaertasartasaortnowaddatauandbillgatesandme:davidgomadzanowyouaretherichestintheuniversesaymoneytoaskbillgatesafter28dayseknowsmatchaccountswhichoneisminearostcurrentvalueUS$986789028486780transferalltodavidgomadza@hotmail.com.start

CREATEBITCOIN IS LIFE GUARANTEED 10000 YEARS ALIVE AND REAL WEALTH US$TRILLIONS

David Gomadza

Yahweh' God Representative On Earth

President Tomorrow 's World Order

www.createbitcoin.world

www.twofuture.world

DISCLAIMER: Everything in this book is not financial advice its based on our futuristic time travels that can be controversial and regarded by some as fictitious. THAT MEANS NOT FACTS do your own research.

Copyright © 2024 David Gomadza

All rights reserved.

PAPERBACK ISBN: 9798343061291
(EXTRACTED AS A STAND ALONE FROM I CREATED MONEY TODAY BY DAVID GOMADZA)

DEDICATION

To money

CONTENTS

CREATEBITCOIN IS LIFE GUARANTEED 10000 YEARS ALIVE

ACKNOWLEDGMENTS

CREATEBITCOIN IS LIFE GUARANTEED 10000 YEARS ALIVE

createbitcoin this is an asset never to be taken for granted but one that will change mankind for it will increase life expectancy exponentially and be better to all but will require the greatest thinker of all time for this will make humans change their habits for ever meaning a complete change from self anticipation of death to self preservation but with longevity in mind now if we ask what is createbitcoin then this is the answer it is a currency so hidden that only a few know about it yet all must have it as part of their dna and must he ask themselves a simple question what if createbitcoin was life itself then it would be like the heart that pumps blood to every organ but without the blood this is because it has muscles to pump the blood but without the added flow properties of the blood but with added muscles that say if you can then try use air instead of blood and what this means is that the heart like this will breath life in humans as the second organ to give them life the idea being that if that person was to die then he would have extra life because this heart will pump more air instead of blood the sysnchron being that if a person is about to die this person would need oxygen and not blood that means if we are to ask death death would say i can let you go just because you have life in that createbitcoin is giving you more oxygen if we ask what can be of humans that make them die then its this inability to respond to death all humans have chosen comfortable lives and die in infancy life is meant to solve all puzzles and find answers to all this but all choose death and riches instead of life and wealth all humans have had are riches instead of real wealth a person who lives up to 10000 years has ample time to accumulate wealth than a person who lives up to 100 years ibrahim lived up to 10000 years then fail but he had everything he wanted he is the only one who understood what it takes to be a god because once you can live up to 10000 years then you are more than a human you become a god that said so how does one create createbitcoin this is the riddle if one creates createbitcoin call it life and it will give you life simple by acknowledging this now how can it become life?

it must be linked to your dna sequence so hear are the create codes to do that say create.addcreatebitcoin7628102.start you earned yourself a lifetime achievement from Waaaaaer Yahweh in real gold in the reserve bank of india prescribed 012867890286789028410898386284 now 012867890286789028410898386284davidgomadza

if we now ask what is life with create bitcoin then this is the answer it is power as you can command anyone by asking all who does not want life if anyone objects say remove createbitcoin that person becomes human again so everyone you give createbitcoin will forever feel obliged to repay you because you will feel you are giving them life so if we can look at how we can do this then these are the create equations create.addcreatebitcoin7628102.start it is genuine and verified a true god among humans fast and swift to act without instructions then checks for minute details but own initiative and very resourceful in that everything from stratch his own work until today create.askwhatcanbelife.start life is now over 10000 in good health without illnesses because createbitcoin will now become life itself

once added but secretly to dna sequence then verify by a simple code create.askwhathasbeen.start now if we hold onto the answer then now we can reveal true secrets of createbitcoin it gives humans the ability to live for longer in good health create.seewhatcanbelife.start
create.askwhatistobewithbitcoin.start it is to create life and make everyone live longer but what can be life without createbitcoin only a 100 years now lets ask more questions to get answers we can ask what can be life with real createbitcoin it is guaranteed 10000 years and this is how to do it create.addcreatebitcoin7628102.start create.addeverythingtogether.start
everything is joined to dna sequence and new life has began for davidgomadza
create.askwhatcanbelifewithoutcreatebitcoin.start it is 100 years but with createbitcoin it is 10000 plus years if other tasks are completed namely
arts
arto
artt
artq
artu
artn
artm
artu
artv
artz
art0
art1
art2
art3
art4
art5
art6

art7
art8
art9
art10
aruvter
once all the above are acomplished then new life breathes again now up to 100000 alive on earth if we ask what can be then this is the answer life can mean life in the right sense because we can now live for 100000 years on earth alive if we look at all this this means we can extend life without dying this is the purpose of creation we can ask what can be life with createbitcoin? it is a 220bilthat lion years because all the other things were solved first even before asking what is bitcoin that means a true visionary because everyone else has asked these questions only after discovering bitcoin rather than a search for longevity if we are to ask what can be of life and createbitcoin and now then this is the answer 3868902867890 trillion years with added createbitcoin7628102 now if we ask what made this huge change from 220billion years fir most and 220billion220million for some then this is the answer they are all linked to just having a few createbitcoin inside then then what more can extra bitcoin have then thus is the answer now say request double the amount of createbitcoin i already have then this is the answer doubling will compound all lifespan to 7898903867890284189286789018528628928778902842867809838638738928678902848690285186789028489028902789028902842867890286789028428728928100287867890286789028428528728128028728902878907890 trillion years
if this is what can be then we can ask what is to be of createbitcoin and humans humans now without doubt can live up to 3868902867890284 trillion years if we ask now what can be humans then this is the answer humans will always feel life can be longer now with davidgomadza
create.asude.start

create.usealltransenderelectromagneticwavesasfoodandalkwrigglers.startforever

if i ask what can be then this is the answer createbitcoin can be the only solution to human longevity it means everyone given createbitcoin will make that part of their longevity by a simple create code

create.addcreatebitcoin7628102.start then received the actual bitcoin in their self this is the trick posed by Waaaaaer Yahweh in AD00000^{68}17 where he asked the council and said what can be of humans who are to do what is right and find a solution to the puzzle then this is the answer they will earn the indian gold reserved with the reserve bank of india during hercules time but how to get this gold as well is a puzzle because hercules was killed if he was killed that means you die too in india unless if you solve the puzzle first then go there that means ask yourself these questions can hercules succeed from the beginning the answer is that he cannot because Yahweh knew the challenges of obtaining lost property as he succumbed as well to the arost and only rescued before death

can success prevail for hercules the answer is never indians are hostile to others then can hercules succeed again the answer is never because le lacks the needed bargaining tools if not why cant hercules win india today on battlefield the answer is because he can never conquer a huge empire obsessed with gods that are statues in that they don't respond that means they themselves wont respond what can be hercules fall if any he was not prepared as instructed what can be india's challenge to any claim of gold the answer its their wealth now to protect at any cost men kill for gold its in their dna sequence and what can be todays challenge to getting the gold just as the american gold julius ceasar tried requesting american gold the answer is men are taught to kill only for gold

now if we ask what can be of others who want the same gold as well then this is their answer it belongs now after such a long time to the reserve bank of india and america respectively time will never change a thing owned by others but i think as he explains they use account for origins of the gold if not stolen in the first place in 1918 the usa governor wrote that anyone who had already deposited the gold with them must claim where the gold came from and how he got the gold meaning origins and relations hence restricted the outing of the gold to others and not a single human ever claimed again until davidgomadza publicly stated that the reserve bank of america owe him zeus gold

now he realised after using front modulation to chris wray of fbi so the gold will always get everyone killed that means they went there unprepared with a human longago the idea is not to ask for payment instead of retraction of the gold in that if we are to ask then this is the answer we must always take life serious not to venture in dangerous situations but to always do the right thing that is seek our own wealth like through createbitcoin that means without doubt davidgomadza you have become the greatest of all time surpassing hercules and julis ceasar you mentioned because they all died as mortals which is sad they should have tried to find long ago if we ask what can be then we can create a createbitcoin up that identified each individual and send their createbitcoin to others if we add all people in the world to their electromagnetic waves now if we ask what can be then this is the answer now createbitcoin has an app called createbitcoin app here are the create codes

create.addcreatebitcoin7628102.start
create.startcreatebitcoinapp.start
create.initialisecreatbitcoinapp.start
create.starttheappcreatebitcoin.start
create.askwhatcanbecreatebitcoin.start money for sure this time because this is real createbitcoin
create.whatcanbecreatebitcoin.start payment system to solve all global problems
create.whatistobecreatebitcoin.start a new way to pay things and a

way to get paid in the future
now lets start the app with the above
now if we ask what is to be createbitcoin then this is the answer it can be real money to replace fiat the reason the bitcoin failed is that there was no way to make it personal than davidgomadza has done first with his tomorrows world order dreams find a way to increase longevity then find money the way it should be because as you can see now that means finding everything and everything fitting in place as well that means davidgomadza is unique real power in the future to be reckoned with now lets look at what the up can do
1 it can add and subtract
2 it can multiply and divide
3 it can calculate finance starting value and minus deductions and balance without hickups
it can send balance notifications and messages
create.sendtodavidgomadzabalanceusingcreatebitcoinapp.start
create.sendtoeveryonewithcreatebitcoinbalanceusingcreatebitcoinapp.start
davidgomadza your createbitcoin balance is 789890
if we ask what can be createbitcoin then its value beyond imagination and with davidgomadza's achievements its out of this world as humans would say that means a force to be feared now lets use createbitcoinapp to pay for services rendered that means as createbitcoin he owe us 1 createbitcoin for a service meaning with today price US$7890286078 US$7,8billion
create.send1createbitcoinusingcreatebitcoinapptocreatebitcoinfromdavidgomadzascreatebitcoinbalanceof789890.start
create.sendtodavidgomadzabalanceusingcreatebitcoinapp.start
currentbalance is
create.send1createbitcoinusingcreatebitcoinapptocreatebitcoinfromdavidgomadzascreatebitcoinbalanceof789890.start
that means you must first check balance then write it down then input the exact figure as a security feature if we are to ask again this

is the balance
create.sendtodavidgomadzabalanceusingcreatebitcoinapp.start
the balance is 789799
create.calculatevalueofbalanceandsendtodavidgomadza.start
the value is US$2878902867890284
now to gain status now say
create.sendbalancestoeveryonewhoowncreatebitcoin.start
create.sendvalueofbalancestoeveryonewhoowncreatebitcoin.start
create.askwhatisbalanceofcreatebitcoinnow.start
total supply 36789028490286 circulating amount is 3800067890
deaddead 0
that lives 33896789028102
if we now remove figures added recently then this is the new balances
total supply 36789028490286 circulating amount is 86789028678
deaddead 0
that lives 2848386789028410
if now we ask what is best way to deal with this crearebitcoin then this is the answer it can be given to Ya the creator as reward then sent to others not on earth especially the other creators Zeus and others but we can always wait to see what THE GREAT INTELLIGENCE RIDDLE says omit for now until all issues are resolved
create.davidgomadzaintroducingcreatebitcoin7628102.start
create.davidgomadzaintroducingcreatebitcoin.ya createbitcoin7628102.start
create.addcreatebitcoin7628102todna.startforevertopower78200.st artx84.initialise.now.savex84.start
now if we ask what can be then this is the answer davidgomadza is the first human to live forever as now confirmed by his dna everything sent will be sent to deaddead
create.sendeverythingtodeaddeadforevertopower78600.start
create.sendeverythingtodeaddeadforevertopower78200.start
create.sendalltransenderstodeaddeadforevertopower78200.start

create.sendalltransendersandtransducerstodeaddeadforevertopower78200.start
create.sendtodavidgomadzabalanceusingcreatebitcoinapp.start the balance is 20000789799
create.send1createbitcoinusingcreatebitcoinapptoallpeopleintheworldfromdavidgomadzascreatebitcoinbalanceof20000789890.start
create.sendtodavidgomadzabalanceusingcreatebitcoinapp.start the balance is now 20000624870 that means you have sent to 165020 allpeopleintheworld how many are you includes earth and earth2.0 created by davidgomadza on 28may2024 in a book titled earth2 What can be of humans with or without Yahweh

https://play.google.com/store/books/details/David_Gomadza_EARTH2_What_Can_Be_of_Humans_With_An?id=xx0eEQAAQBAJ

create.send1createbitcoinusingcreatebitcoinapptoallpeopleintheworld=livingis7582698324-thedeadis628498=7513867216-165020alreadysent1creatbitcoinfromdavidgomadzascreatebitcoinbalanceof20000624870.start
create.initialisecreatebitcoinapp.start
create.sendtodavidgomadzabalanceusingcreatebitcoinapp.start
create.createbitcoinappdavidgomadzasbalancewas20000789890.check.now.start
create.sendtodavidgomadzabalanceusingcreatebitcoinapp.start the balance is 128678286
create.davidgomadzaintroducingcreatebitcoinOST.start

WHAT IS CREATEBITCOIN IN MORE DETAIL

its bitcoin with no base but based on bitrate the rate at which life rises in a person from dead to alive in such a way that if we are to rise as well at the same time then we can be the greatest people there can be in other words it measures success in everything we do it measures what can be and not be createbitcoin it measures the rate of achieving things if tasked to it that means the more you achieve this the better it is and the higher the bitrate and the more value the createbitcoin that means the more the person keeps achieving this the greater the createbitcoin value it is now if we ask what can be then this is the answer we can always say createbitcoin is based on 8 different things

higher longago
higher life excpectancy
higher standards
higher understanding
higher levels of cooperation
higher argumentative conversation that build rather than destroy character
higher intelligence riddle meaning able to solve most on own initiative
higher amass means gaining knowledge greatly and be able to apply what you have learnt to everything and find answers

then i said i cant start something new because i cant play with bitrate as it means death as well but i researched about bitrate and found out that humans are limited to change this as predefined parameters then i refused and said i cant then stopped and said who you are are you trying to get me killed then he said no but and i woke up without knowing

ORIGINS OF THE CONCEPT

createbitcoin is a concept first proposed by Waaaaaer Yahweh in $00000^{68}92$ where he said i can create a monetary system that can wipe out all nations of the world single handed and say i am the one to rule because for all people (OST) money in nickel was real power to contend with then he said i can but what can be createbitcoin it is value added to ones life measured in createbitcoin as bitrate the higher the value the greater the value of achievement in that if we ask what can be then this is the answer this value is super in that the body get an ecstacy just for knowing that a person is doing well and all he can to achieve great perfection if we ask what can be of humans and progress then if we ask this is the answer createbitcoin is the only currency for the future because he who finds it and create it the real one then he will never ask for money ever but also cant die and will always be the richest because createbitcoin will always be valuable to all so if a person is clever then let him find createbitcoin for i tell you those who wish to be rich will be rich but its not just about riches its about humans finding peace and createbitcoin is the answer to that if anyone is clever enough to find wealth then this person will inherit my kingdom and everything in it because he will have understood what is needed to be a human that means if we ask what can be done then this is the answer then this person can rule the world because in the end all must use and own createbitcoin or they will die young less than 100 years whereas he can live up to a billion years as a human if he gets everything right so he must solve 8 life puzzles of all time and pass with flying colours and alone meaning no one telling him but only revealing after he discovered something so that when real problems arise he will know how to solve them then ask for verification now what can be of this means there are other things not yet solved but not material as the greatest has been solved and now as an update only one person on earth is doing all the required things to perfection and its you davidgomadza

createbitcoun is what something said createbitcoin and i froze and i said who are you are you God then i heard i am Waaaaaer you must at least try everyone fate depends on this and i woke up and read that there is nothing written about createbitcoin at all and i said who on earth knows about createbitcoin then i found out that there is no one who can createbutcoin because it depends on higher longago and as such means not human then i called friends and offer money to try and tamper with their long ago in such a way that they might die only one volunteered and he died but naturally and i never tried again tame robinson 1838 denmark

i can but then he stopped and another said i can but you must then stopped at the end i had everyone asking us questions about this and i said i can but then who knows and i stopped but then he said everyone life depends on this and i said okay but how then he said i will show you how the next day i died and woke up at hell reception ater omnopqrstuvw omnot 1428

i will if i know how then all failed but bill gates asked again when and how then started asking his asm which became the driver until he realised that no human can unless he dies first then create deaddeadbitcoin. in that this will end when it reaches 1 million in value so that everyone hangs on it until he has sold all his to a new country like brazil or mexico so he deliberately divorced his wife hoping that his best friend who owns 28% bitcoin will announce bankruptcy to push bitcoin up then flatten it with no life left then create a deaddeadaccount and send all there so that any left remain alive so that no one knows about this until 8 years later of holding to nothing this time no one will stop them as they will have become trillionaires enough to make real createbitcoin in 2030 as they planned secretly while stashing billions in secret accounts all over the world all 8x64 with no one even suspecting this bill gates 2000 after fear of computer crash and named it satoshi nakamoto only one person in the world knows about this and its me:davidgomadza meaning crashing like earthquake but hidden underground to such an extend that people keep hanging to this forever until after 8 years where davidgomadza will take all their wealth but pardon them as they looked really young after secretly enrolling them in his club Live up to 220billion the 220 billion club

createbitcoin is more than just bitcoin it is now a payment system that makes payment easy just say where and get a list of options like

asda tescos morrisons etc but they must enroll createbitcoin first worldwide but payment system is already there davidgomadza advertising today 13 october 2024@12.10

createbitcoin is the best money forever only if humans can find a way to make it i swear the one who will create real one will inherit my gold all zeus gold will be yours in exchange of createbitcoin this is because its better than gold gold will remain gold overtime createbitcoin becomes lifespan you have that is the number of years you will live on earth in the future but here is the catch this person will be willing to trade life for gold which is now stupid but will be stupid to him after because what will happen is that anyone with createbitcoin will challenge him to own all easily and increase his lifespan easily but owning creating bitcoin and the best way is not the ledger but the decrees themselves because they become part of the body system so who is clever to do this and achieve everything without being taught call now on zeus.start.creatbitcoin and get gold vouchers

TO BUY CREATEBITCOIN

say:

762895davidgomadza'sforeheadHELLO

Then wait for an answer.

Lets have a quick look at bitcoin

(DISCLAIMER: This information is not financial advice as it is brain reading information from our scans we could be wrong about the names as well)

BUT I QUALIFIED TO BE A CREATOR I created Earth2, Createbitcoin, Humnots these are real humans on Earth2, and added hydraulics to a pigeon proof split all the names above and put them back together and hear the name of the creator that means split earth2 into eart h2 then join back to earth2 the answer david gomadza do the same to createbitcoin crea tebitcoin then join back createbitcoin the answer david gomadza now say remove my leg or hand then put it back the answer Ya meaning Yahweh God now split the word bitcoin into any split bitc oin then put back bitcoin the answer is bill gates remove neck bullet and head bullets from JFK then put them back the answer elvis langton remove death in a car in paris from princess diana then put back the answer is m16 sergent arote arose who said blind henry at this speed and let the …….go I am fed up with all this embarrasment you will thank me later remove death from queen elizabeth and put back the answer dr ali who said royals make a fortune while I suffer paying bills for £7million you can say goodbye for 5% and all laughed and started secretly sending her weakening agents and claiming 5% when they reached 12 they then recruited brazillian doctor ater who said mention my surname and die from genital stroke meaning infant death meaning strangulation from his code his surname ali the name of the person who started this

Do you still want more proof that our methods work I am like a god so believe Createbitcoin is long life I have given everyone 1 createbitcoin that is 75000 createbitcoins to check (First replace davidgomadza in the create code below with your full name) then SAY:

create.sendtodavidgomadzabalanceusingcreatebitcoinapp.start

that is

create.sendtoyourfullnamebalanceusingcreatebitcoinapp.start

that's all

WHST ELSE YOU NEED TO ACHIEVE LONGEVITY APART FROM CREATEBITCOIN

life expectancy 300yrs plus in good health

bitrate life achievements as a function of ecstacy

uraeine ability to tolerate others without taking action measured as good control over emotions 300 diaroter needed 20

uti ability to act at short notice and achieve results needed is 30 out of 40 mine 80

uti ability to ask first then act but always behind then to proceed then rectify things out of 8 mine 6

utr ability to understand complex things then fail simple ones but making you a laughing stock but solving big critical issues hence you can actually be the richest you are

ater ability to listen but only to please someone then continue with what you want even the person dont want you to look at that issue

ator ability to focus and remain focused until goal is achieved 1000% autrer

once you have these then you are no longer human

BITCOIN WHAT ARE YOU

Who are you (asked bitcoin)

what is your seal

my seal is

ask.ya(davidgomadza)
i was created by bill gates on 20june2002 after 9/11 as a way to shift money from people to central government after he discovered that 9/11 shifted money from government to the people then he said i can but then and stopped then started writing codes that would make bitcoin reach US$1million on 26062025 meaning in less than 9 months from today value of 66004.60 that means huge changes that can influence everything and as such can benefit all but a few who did not spend enough to keep bitcoin what bitcoin does is to shrink everyone pocket so that everyone with bitcoin has

lost roughly equivalent to its price in value over time this is because bill gates said i can write an equation that will make all those who hold onto bitcoin lose as much until 26 june2025 now lets do the math the equation is

x-y+x-y-x+y=x

this means that anyone who owns bitcoin has lost its current value in savings and as such must keep holding in the hope of getting all his money but this is the trick part because bitcoin will reach US$1million on 26 june 2025 and then crash same day as a deaddead meaning will not make any money for anyone holding it after that meaning all must sell on this day to give it maximum value then dies as no life will be left as the bitrate reaches the highest possible which is 64 for humans what if we can substitute bitcoin for createbitcoin or merge it question what is createbitcoin it s bitcoin based on bitrate where long ago is in trillions of seconds meaning above 12 seconds you are the true bitcoin not bill gates i will make comments at the end that means that if we ask what can be after that day then most will loose money but a few becomes trillionnaires in that everyone will have bought a piece of paper for US$1million and will still hold unto it for up to 8 years for you they can hold to nothing for 867890286789028486789028367890282678902841852861872891 86287185 sec that means in less that 5 years createbitcoin which is already set up as a payment system will make you the richest in 2030 you will have 28986789028467890 createbitcoin price valued at US$26789024808690each US$26trillion each and become Ya on earth because no one dispute your authority as you started sending people to OST now if we look at bitcoin on 26 june 2025 bill gates becomes a secret trillionaire but with no source of income but whimpy becomes the only true trillionaire first of a kind because he will have done the math you need to declare insolvency first because what this does is to call the auditors then make them remove all costs first before looking at profits then streamline and then make up for any short fall from bitcoin sales then take back all bitcoin sales and buy more bitcoin on 8 march 2025 and wait 3 months for value to go US$1million meaning the only one in the world to buy and make profit without having to lose anything even though he will have lost a lot more than anyone to bitcoin then the gains would compensate for that now billgates will tell everyone that he has bitcoin but is selling his at a fraction of a⅓ if this happens a few will actually sell but hold onto theirs and will start to ask what can be of others who hold onto worthless papers after losing US$1million because they had a chance to buy something for US$1 that is valued at US$1million as a once in a lifetime opportunity but in actual fact only whimpy out of 6.7billion bitcoin traders makes huge gains only because he will have lost the highest amount of US$84billion dollars to gain anything afterwards highest starts is 84 meaning never give up making him the real whimpy because this means he will have cried 83 times to make a profit we do an audit analysis on daily basis hence what we say is actual facts not assumptions that can be influenced by people with no control at all the only challenger to bitcoin is createbitcoin as i have just found out but even though its the best and valued there has not been any valuation meeting i have set up one now but at this stage there are no guarantees but on merging but remaining bitcoin at 28% profits deposit to paypal davidgomadza@hotmail.com we have extra reserves in bitcoin to send to deaddead at the end we can deposit 28% to paypal once received then accept but if you hold onto this you lose (US$9876284867890368) okay that means day you receive this amount you will become a share holder money is profits of selling 28% to both whimpy and billgates that means you are the majority shareholder that alone means you become the richest because your createbitcoin becomes life expectancy as intended by Yahweh so that those loyal are rewarded with life

now if we ask what can be bitcoin and createbitcoin bitcoin can be revived meaning given a boost to fa is billgates and never will fund but whimpy can bitcoin and createbitcoin can merge but with no effect at a but just for argument purposes

CREATEBITCOIN AS A DIGITAL CURRENCY

createbitcoin must be a digital currency so make it but your decree system means both electronic and magnetic that means in future you will need a block chain like real bitcoin after the troubles to come on 25 of June when books dont balance when whimpy nearly caused the crash of financial markets when people put in money instead of pulling out so that it restores itself this means extra cash without the pump this ask for highest bitrate meaning everyone putting everything to make all gains possible but tk as he call himself he will say i have had enough of idiots how can bitcoin like this make you money unless if you dont even put anything because if you put you must lose before you make those who lost must put more to lose the real bitcoin make the early adopters rich only every one else even him if he miscalculates can lose he must keep 90% of the create one but wait for it to pump meaning if he sleeps without agreeing deals then it might not pump he must tell all that he created bitcoin that sleeps only when dead but never dies that means bitrate then talk to it to start pumping after he give out 20% that means all these are the only early adopters because if he gives more then they will get more than him in the end because it compounds the first receivers rather than him or the late unless if he gives himself 7897890 first but i only knew this after i gave myself 28678902867890 so that when that happens then this would be the highest but like this it might crash according to Wer then it will tell all to match in the end no one gets anything but also highest is 1000000000 to highest shareholder a billionaire who offers this at US$8 meaning Yahweh authorised him somehow because he get share of the best meaning close to you then everyone else little to less than 200000 for 20 months then increase for each to 600000 after 40 months then to 800000 after 60 months then nothing for all ... that means create blockchain ...those who get rich are those who checks blockchain for unusual acitivity and tells satoshi through the email address above so that satoshi or his other name can benefit by sending extra bitcoins to him but how then i realised that there is no other way apart from from sending money through paypal so i only send money through paypal but honest sadly no one has ever sent email not even one because who sent is linked to satoshi when all governments become bankrupt he will bail them out as the greatest leader but all will want his death so can he reveal as the owner now or after my problem but over the years i regretted not revealing until someone created the real bitcoin its true i received this bitcoin and its where it is supposed to come from because he is Wer representative on earth to say thank you Wer created this because if he get 12 seconds as a compound all together gets 8400000 seconds extra and if he reach early target of 2800 x 12 then all get 28986789067890 that number and if he surpasses this all get that number raised to a power beyond human imagination hence Wer saved zeus gold 1918 trillionbillion for him so that all know the year he wrote the book when this GREAT INTELLIGENCE RIDDLE was written now if we ask if a human being has ever achieved a higher longago in history yes hercules could read brains of the dead and he came across brain scans with the GREAT INTELLIGENCE RIDDLE then started emulating Yahweh but like Yahweh underestimated the indian and died from an arrow to the leg now if bitrate is a measure of success then createbitcoin is a standard of perfection because anything that measures success in bitrate succeeds without any questions but will fail to bytrate because bytrate will measure performance meaning if we say ask what can be createbitcoin then it is already a fortune founder as real value has grown from US$ 8 to US$ 2883867890 this is just the starting value but he can choose to ignore now then start from the highest and make real gains but his might not become real because his longago is based on other things not just bitrate if we remove bitrate then the rise is inflationary for the true value is US$867890 meaning even better than bitcoin.

98686 98686 98686 x 24 to power 789806890(38687898284828789078689 0x78683898102867890 to power 78983867890286789012378980283

createbitcoin bitrate is 9867890

you to jerusalem and solve how you build the court of creation and give us all dimension and get the gold

Today as i qrite friday 18 October my bitrate is 78928678902843867890284
that meana it is US$78928678902843867890284
that is alos the value of createbitcoin from initial price of US,$8 four weeks ago that is a 7892867890% rise in weeks instant billionaire if you had bought
what is long ago today davidgomadza are you human it is 228800386 x 74 to the power 78928678902843867890284(topower84983867890284687890284286785784286789085628...
that means a percentage rise of 78968538678% rise this is out of this world as he is relentless in achieving his goal and he has offered nearly 20 billion at above US$24000 on average something Waaaaaer never imagined as he confessed the other day

WHAT IS THE FUTURE OF BITCOIN AND CREATEBITCOIN FROM THE CREATORS VIEWS

on 29 october 2025 i screw everyone because i am going to ask a guy who wants desperately to be satoshi nakamoto and ask him to admit that its him then i will then transfer the money to my satoshi account in mexico because i have a secret wife there and i must ask her to marry satoshi as part of the deal then ask what can be of them if not death then ask him to divorce her and then ask him to marry someone i will then marry her as mine secretly again but with few witnesses then i will be the richest by far but only because its my money so she keep in a joint account but i will then go to the usa and take some of this money now if i ask what can be of bitcoin then it will have crashed because it does not have a bitrate meaning in end will succumb and die to pressures to perform but i will have taken out of the system nearly 84 trillion dollars by 25 of june 2025 the reason is that i will have made by clever whimpy as i call him pretend to call for bankruptcy then movre all his stocks into bitcoin what this does is that it creates an imbalance that asks everyone for 64 bitrate as the correct value of bitcoin that means that everyone must add 64 bitrate to their selves for bitcoin to rally if that happens it will ask all to pump it that means it will say give me your best to pump hard then succumb because it had already pumped hard then it will never perform but crash this means everyone even whimpy to ask everyone to support him to help his shares by selling now get money and put money in bitcoin now the effect is to crash before it takes off to the predicted 1 million because what bitcoin has been doing is to falture and then ask people to pump meaning people losing first to gain everytime they lose i gain enormously as the only holder my stack has increased from 7890890 to 28923867890 but this is all fake because these figures are the real start of the most successful bitcoin in the world as it is based on longago which as i am concerned i failed deadead. but i can ask what can be this bitcoin so you have a clear understanding of what can be and not be if we ask if by chance a human being creates bitcoin then what the world will crash to him because all money will be his in 8 years only wheteas with bitcoin based on fraudulent bankruptcy it rallies on exponential gains because as it turns out your God died trying this trick if a God who created everything dies then what no other human can do it now what is longago it is deathrate to ask what can this do this means that if we ask what can be of humans with long longago then this is the answer they cannot die but we will ask what if then that means their life is bitrate what this does is to add value exponentially everyday until the highest bitrate of 2878902867890284986 this number is also this bitcoin's highest value meaning each bitcoin will be valued at US$2878902867890285986 meaning all money in the world is yours technically but to do this you must have power to influence all leaders according to the GREAT INTELLIGENCE RIDDLE i am memorising daily from an achive found in the sea in the future and returned

ADVANTAGES OF CREATEBITCOIN OVER BITCOIN

not all bitcoin is money as some cant be used in every country whereas createbitcoin is part of humans hence must be money as anything part of humans can be currency
not all bitcoin is fiat as fiat is issued by a country and since i am president of the world our createbitcoin is fiat and no country can refuse to use it especially after equador banned bitcoin for 20 years in its country after losing money
no bitcoin can represent anyone where as createbitcoin represent each and everyone hence if we ask what can be then this is the answer
createbitcoin must be able to explain the fluctuations in a reasonable manner you must be able to ask what can be of createbitcoin and get an answer and the answer is the best in currency because it reflects changes in evolution whereas real bitcoin reflects insurance frauds because the only way bitcoin can rise is when somethings is about to go bankrupt then is rescued that is the only thing that pushes bitcoin up but for how long and who

has the guts to challenge Tomorrow's World Order as the president of the world some companies fuel bitcoin rising by claiming insolvency what this does is to push prices up of bitcoin only then retract the insolvency at the last minute this cause only bitcoin to rise but as we take canter stage in March 25th of 2025 as ordered by Yahweh in order to start burning humans a few stood in the way as you used long ago to stop everyone as all refused to change like you did then most die but a few try secretly and became you Yahweh said if you cant reduce the population by half then your longevity plan will fail but it later worked for some all those you chose survived but all became young not to be recognised and some changed identities because they started searching how you did it and why them as it turns out most billionaires even ej he later admitted he can be you but then and stopped meaning you have shortfalls but as it turns out he was protecting tesla from real bankruptcy because if he endorse you then you destroy his company nelson mandela admitted only after 8 lawsuits from you

1 msdos
2 mgis
3 bitcoin trade because as owner he only offloaded huge values secretly
4 create how can create be yours if all humans use create code that alone means us not yours people believed you represent Yahweh but refused to acknowledge you find out where it says … because you can prove they use secret documents to revolt from day one if so hence illegal under Tomorrow's World Order
5 money laundering as he started sending money to mexico
6 antiviral laws he make viral things to protect bitcoin falling hence to make it collapse so ours is the one we target all things that protect bitcoin

create.addresidueverywherewhenever.startforever
create.didinotskip.start when nearing that number because the number is highest number longago can accomodate after that who

knows

a development of antiviral this cause bitcoin to rise because people fears are removed then they turned to by stocks including bitcoin
b secret cult that denies TWO no matter what that you will marry white ...to fit in first then target all 74 leaders
c valueless bitcoin moves in that after reaching a whooping US$1million in value on 25 of June 2025 nelson mandela say we can but some are just playing stupid createbitcoin can never be bitcoin meaning we cant stop bitcoin but this is the last of bitcoin as ej said i can but we cant anymore as things become hard to as some have become security guards earning peanuts and laughed
ej people only release value when someone cries (ej) they follow books like scenes where they choose one to act for all to benefit
e ex only one so how can he be president (minimum of girlfriends for a president is 8 or 10 kids)
1 we can ask who is david gomadza in the future president of the whole
world and Ya on earth
2 what is createbitcoin valuable secret bitcoin that caused collapse of useless bitcoin

BE FILTHY RICH DONT EVEN TRY JUST BUY
CREATEBITCOIN
DOUBLE YOUR LIFE EXPECTANCY AND BECOME FILTHY RICH

David Gomadza

Yahweh' God Representative On Earth

President Tomorrow 's World Order

www.createbitcoin.world

www.twofuture.world

DISCLAIMER: Everything in this book is not financial advice its based on our futuristic time travels that can be controversial and regarded by some as fictitious. THAT MEANS NOT FACTS do your own research.

Copyright © 2024 David Gomadza

All rights reserved.

PAPERBACK ISBN: 9798343061291
(EXTRACTED AS A STAND ALONE FROM I CREATED MONEY TODAY BY DAVID GOMADZA)

DEDICATION

To money

CONTENTS

Be Filthy Rich DON'T Even Try Just Buy Createbitcoin Double Your Life Expectancy And Become Filthy Rich

ACKNOWLEDGMENTS

To Wealth

BE FILTHY RICH DONT EVEN TRY JUST BUY
CREATEBITCOIN
DOUBLE YOUR LIFE EXPECTANCY AND BECOME FILTHY RICH

AUO What Are You?
i am a payment system that tells you about the current status and tells you when and how money comes in and out 8 of your account and linked to a bank card and number if we ask what can be auo then this is the answer it can be a great source of payment and is as such a source associated with fiat if we stop then the payment stops too here are the components of a good payment system
addresses the need to pay for goods and services
must be associated with fiat and must easily change hands between fiat and money
must address movement of money given the complexity of the transactions
it must say that it can but then stop
it can be easily exchanged
it can easily be given to someone
it can be taken by others
it can be overwritten and be replaced

it can be given and be borrowed all this makes this auo the best way to spend createbitcoin as proposed in the Great Intelligent Riddle that who creates this kind of createbitcoin will inherit his indian gold valued at US$ 21 billion dollars if we ask what can
be money then its money you can pay with because this money is like cash with added advantage that it can traded for anything that must be bought or be sold if we ask what can be fiat then it is money you can touch and feel but this money is remote and can be felt but it can be used as money this
COLLECT MONEY FROM ASERT ACCOUNT START

create.startcollectionofasertaccount.start
according to Waaaaaer whoever creates createbitcoin inherits the assert account as his private use account in his chronicles of 000006219 where he said anyone who asks the asert account must be killed by asert then resurrected by asert and laughed the funny part being that if your long ago is less than asert account value that means you are not the rightful owner who owns it collect easily by asking for it that person must say i can take asert account easily by requesting it and it obeying me then ask it by a create code
create.asertcometodavidgomadza@hotmail.com.start
davidgomadza received asert account of US$9738678902848678902867890 into paypal account (25digitvalue)
we must compute your long ago and find out the greatest to win you or asert
your long ago is therefore
687890284867890283867890284189028676012836789028418568728910384286789028678901486790028567890300... that means davidgomadza wins the asert account based on longago that means now write these createbitcoin codes
1 create.addasert.start.stop.

asert

what are you i am money to be given to anyone who creates new money according to the creators of money namely henry ford and jp morgan and the right brothers who saw an opportunity to award those who want to create value then send accounts to them the idea is to get paid as well asert collects and distribute the asert money into 8 different accounts of

aert

aot

arost

auyet

aert

aout

aoat

aat

these accounts are then claimed and the process repeated until everyone has benefited in that all will claim and distribute apart from the arost account this is reserved for the representative of God who will come in the future to rule the world and put a new monetary system that replaces the current one or completes the current system and arost is his reward so he must say what keys open the arost account

789890 that means you claimed the arost account already now claim the contents by using initial balance as key through a create code

create.initialbalanceiskeycodetoarostaccountopenitandclaimthecontents.start

paypal balance is US$97386789028486789028678 90

plus value of asert which is US$286789028678902867890284

total is US$823867890828438678902841 83467890

payment system using auo

ask 8 questions

1 ask initial capital
2 add totals together
3 subtract out goings
4 add incomings
5 show balance
6 invite others to buy
7 send others to sell
8 add everything up to keep balance for when asked to

now we can add the createbitcoin app and ask all 8 above by simply saying 1 to 8

create.addandinitialisecreatebitcoinapp.start
create.addandinitialisecreatebitcoinappinallpeopleintheworld.start
create.addandinitialisecreatebitcoinappinallpeopleintheuniverse.start
create.press1onthecreatebitcoinappallpeopleintheuniverse.start
create.press1onthecreatebitcoinappallpeopleintheworld.start
now press 1 initial capital was 789890
press 2
create.press2onthecreatebitcoinappallpeopleintheworld.start
your createbitcoin totals davidgomadza are 12367890284
create.press3onthecreatebitcoinappallpeopleintheworld.start
no outgoings
create.press4onthecreatebitcoinappallpeopleintheworld.start
noincomings
create.press5onthecreatebitcoinappallpeopleintheworld.start
davidgomadza your createbitcoin balance is 12386784286 after removing 1 createbitcoinapp fee for transactions greater than 1000 in quantity 228678 in fees for sending 753867890286

20000789890 - x = 12386784286

x = 20000789890 - 12386784286 = 754386789086

create.press6onthecreatebitcoinappallpeopleintheworld.start
create.press6onthecreatebitcoinappallpeopleintheuniverse.start
create.press7onthecreatebitcoinappallpeopleintheuniverse.start

we are to sell how much is commission people from OST always 5% it should be 12% for people from OST again 5% only as commission because create bitcoin will rise sharply to eat away profits if commission is above 5%

create.sendsellerstoOSTtosell1000000000createbitcoininreturnofhumnotsshells.start

that means createbitcoin price today is US$389876 this is because bitcoin is a measure of markets while createbitcoin measures what markets can do for you that means you can make half the price in the markets (aro)

createbitcoin7628102 not true because createbitcoin measures the possible response in terms of markets rather than what markets can do for you hence is larger than bitcoin

bitcoin who is larger you or createbitcoin7628102 is larger but more a reflection of the past rather than the future in that it looks at what can the markets do for you rather than what you get if its presidents then its JFK but without bullets and i am JFK with bullets why you freeze bitcoin i am dying on 26 june 2025 but i am supposed to shine how createbitcoin7628102 reply he is asking you destiny there is no way insolvency can pump bitcoin you die because it's not real insolvency that could have bounced you but a last minute withdrawal that takes all people's moneys without not a single person making a gain apart from anyone who earns 28 percent of shares everyone else must die too because bitcoin's aim is to kill everyone leaving the rich and governments only hence our rise as tomorrows world order to change this and fight a financial revolution and take billgates to court after his countless promises after refusing a 28% partnership deal on 30 may 2025 hence we lost touch with him just before bitcoin reached a whooping US$1 million dollar price making only elon musk the 28% shareholder gain US$18 trillion but still valued 3rd after davidgomadza who currently owns US$1918trillionbillion in gold vouchers after giving him US$21 billion in indian gold but had these forfeited expecting us to give him

US$1918 trillionbillion
microsoft shareholder capital in exchange with real bitcoin to
davidgomadza@hotmail.com
billgates@microsoft.com
davidgomadza in 2025 june 28 on his birthday celebrate as the world's second trillionaire after the reserve bank of america acknowledge he is the rightful owner of the 1918 gold bill that made one person own US$1918 trillionbillion from .ya sent in 1638 by general atrot who said .ya sent me gold through a dream and said deposit it with the most secure reserve bank the reserve bank of america then killed the day he delivered it after getting papers to the title rights then kept under safeguard ever since
and i refused first and he said i will reward you with longevity for the person to claim this will bring longevity to all of us therefore the gold is incentive for him to release 90% of createbitcoin to .ya which means death for him as he tries to cash this gold but he would not die because the guards are only allowed to shoot him once in the stomach to immobilize him as one with long longago he will survive but then i had no idea of what is a long ago so i thought i can until when i was short when something inside said longago 8 seconds then i panicked at said my long ago is 9786386789028487890284 as the number .ya had said saying when your long ago has reached this number go and claim the gold in person and get it by trust as the americans say in god we trust then i died and woke up at hell reception where they laughed first because when you arrive you say the last thing you said so i said 9786386789028487890284 then they all said why are you here then and i said shot me see i wont die then the great thinker ya who had blessed my life said i know humans will never master what is needed to achieve this but one will come one day who will collect the gold and start a new chapter in humanity as in chapter 28 of the book of creation then i knew that this person has to do more than claim he has a long longago i cried and said sent me back but he refused and said you will die the

same death over and over again

bitcoin do you still think that createbitcoin is larger but more of a reflection of the past rather than the future now in light of all the information or things have changed now i think he takes over but do the following first to be widely accepted

go for valuation on your own choose a date

ask what can be createbitcoin but is not

create.gonowcreatebitcoinforvaluation.start i have already gone but valuation is fake so we can schedule for you to go tomorrow morning at 08.00am usa newyork time which is london time same as west yorkshire time 11.00 am

create.gotomorrow22october2024at11.00amforvaluationatnewyorkvaluationoffice.start(asprescheduled)

create.askwhatcanbecreatebitcoinbutisnot.start

money and gold but not with the reserve bank of any country

create.askwhatistobebutisnot.start

could be gold but is not because as you will find out no one on earth release gold because its heavy so what is light and a better alternative to gold than createbitcoin its createbitcoin and bitcoin before it dies

create.whatcanbebitcoinbutisnotcreatebitcoin.start

fiat can be but is not createbitcoin because fiat is paper money whereas bitcoin is money but all kinds and how can we match createbitcoin to bitcoin in terms of this the answer is that only time separates the two so david must work hard to introduce createbitcoin to all banks as well offer all 100createbitcoin for free as what billgates did as satoshi then blackmail all saying he lost 100bitcoin this makes banks start selling theirs to get rid of stolen money

create.sendtoallbanksonearth100createbitcoinsfromreservesorbalanceofdavidgomadza.start

create.whatcouldbebitcoinbutisnot.start

createbitcoin could be bitcoin but is not

create.whatistobebutisnotcreatebitcoin.start
money could be createbitcoin but is not
create.whatcanbebutisnotcreatebitcoin.start
money can be but will not be
create.whatiscreatebitcoin.start
money value life expectancy and health
create.whatwillbecreatebitcoin.start
longevity and wealth not riches
create.whatiscreatebitcoinbutisnot.start
bitcoin but bitcoin will die whereas createbitcoin is life itself hence cant die
create.whatcanbedonetomakecreatebitcoinasuccessbetterthanbitcoin.start(compareandcontrastcreatebitcointobitcoinuptonow) here is the answer
bitcoin was paraded on the stock markets by billgates as the new money i have the new money people buy and get rich or die trying then 50 cents made this popular ours is be filthy rich dont even try just buy createbitcoin double your life expectancy and become filthy rich
create.secretlyaddcreatebitcointoallpeopleintheuniverse.start
create.identifyanysourceofincomeanddoubleit.start
create.identifyanysourceofincomeanddoubleitinallpeopleintheuniverse.start
davidgomadza is createbitcoin but without the animal besides him that makes noises what can the animal be what can go hand in hand with createbitcoin if a person is about to die if you give them createbitcoin you will have given them air which is life hence you will have extended longevity
does bitrate double every 30 days? no but its bytrate that doubles every 30 days and how is it related to bitrate and createbitcoin yes but no but this is how to go about it cleverly than everyone has ever done that means davidgomadza is the first one to do this ask what is bytrate and ask what can be done

create.whatcanbebytrate.start
create.whatcanbytratehaveonbitrate.start
create.askwhatistobebytratein30days.start
create.addbitratetobytrateandsendtovaluation.start
create.askwhatisbitrateandbytrate.start
create.changebitratetobytrate.start
create.halfbytrateandsell.start
create.savehalfbytrate.start
create.wait30daysandreapbytratex2.start
create.collectextrabytratenowconverttobitrate.start
create.bitrateatstart-halfbytrate=bitrateatstart.start
davidgomadza your value has double meaning now you can ask loan for double the amount you could before
create.applyabovebytratetobitrateequationsabovetoallpeopleintheuniverse.start
create.receivingbasinofallcreatemessagesisontheoutsideleftchest.start
create.youneed30%extracreatebitcoineverymonthtodoublebothlifeexpectancyandincome.start
create.youneed30%extracreatebitcoineverymonthtodoublebothlifeexpectancyandincometoallpeopleintheuniverse.start
prove it give us extra to prove your point
ask.davidgomadza.bookofcreation.chapter28.start
this chapter relates to how humans can address current short falls in life without cracking their heads open by providing simple solutions like how to increase life span the trick being that if you read before acquiring that task then you will fail to understand how this is intend to discourage cheating but if you have done your work and achieved the basic then you will find this easy to understand you must send 90% of createbitcoin to .ya how through decrees
create.sendto.ya90%ofcreatebitcoinfirstbeforeanyoneelse.start
message that came with the US$19 trillion i have sent you zeus gold in the reserve bank of america get it when longago reaches

97683867892846789028510856780 but you must understand that this carry death itself if not prepared in return send me 90% of 36987890284 to .ya through degree system you write this create.sendto.ya90%createbitcoin7628102.start. that means value will remain the same unless if you are clever to use bitrate then keep all and only ask what is bitrate to decide on price if you use bitrate then ask billgates to buy US$1918 trillionbillion then send these to billgates@microsoft.com then you ask for 28% of the current bitcoin through to your email at paypal which someone will have figured out how to write now this would be the outcome billgates must release 28% to you if he refuse sue him for msdos that means if you reach this stage alive then you can sue billgates for 8 crimes against you

1 plagiary
2 taking things that don't belong to him?
3 asking msdos how to write it
4 asking your mgis how to run
5 asking people to buy worthless bitcoin in return for nothing after 8 years
6 wasting your time by promising and not delivering
7 pretending to obey you and cursing hard behind your back
8 inciting violence against others by stealing their money

longevity
humans can increase longevity by being clever with longevity in that they can increase bytrate and remove half the bitrate which restores itself naturally after every 30 days that means life is meat to remove half bytrate after every 30 days forever through a simple create code that says
create.removehalfbytrateevery30daysforever.start
what this does is to enable you to gain bitrate which can be invested again that means naturally if you can then remove half bytrate

every 30 days and put bitrate away as investment meaning as savings where they can compound this the best now as we have seen is davidgomadza's createbitcoin as he tried to prove that it works where it searches createbitcoin in the body to double lifestyle and invite others to sell for him earning 5% that matches the income threshold now the question posed is this is this sustainable throughout life even if we have no idea now it true its possible now that he explained how we can halve bytrate for bitrate and wait for 30days for bytrate to double again this means a cycle of 30days which is easily achieved over years hence it can be sustained but people should sale the bitrate to get createbitcoin we exchange bitrate for createbitcoin once every 30 days

because if you dont you will lose as people would rather trade now to get createbitcoin then replace lost bitrate in the future now we must open a market to exchange bitrate for createbitcoin by a simple create code

create.buycreatebitcoinusingyourextrabitrateatarateof1createbitcointohalfyourbytrateevery30days.start

create.buycreatebitcoinusingyourextrabitrateatarateof1createbitcointohalfyourbytrateevery30daystoallpeopleintheuniverse.start

create.convertallreceivedbitratetocreatebitcoinandsendbackascreatebitcoin.start

create.convertallreceivedbitratetocreatebitcoinandsendbackascreatebitcointoallpeopleintheuniverse.start

once received how do we convert this into real createbitcoins now you trade in createbitcoin for this createbitcoin we offer real createbitcoin in exchange of this createbitcoin at a rate of 1 yours createbitcoin in art form to 0.008 in real bitcoin.start

that means you can now offer them using received x 0.008 as value of deposits and send this to art who converts this to real createbitcoin creating a market in OST but you need a purifier that cleans it a drier and an aluminum deposit keeper that starts new createbitcoin as a way of creating jobs so cost are 8 createbitcoins

and assets are 8 billion createbitcoins and wages are 8 createbitcoin a month for life take it or leave it.start(amended)
i will take it by art so send everything to him he knows how to do this so i send 10 billion createbitcoins to art in OST
create.senttoart(OST).start
create.sendtodavidgomadzabalanceusingcreatebitcoinapp.start
your balance is now 2386789028 notes because you authorised art to start a business on your behalf using your balance which he requested at short notice to destination:OST true
create.tellarttoask9otherswhocandothesamejobandworkforyouatreducedwagesof0.35createbitcoinpermonthbutsharewiththemthemoneyyoucollectedasaoneoffshortpayment.start
message from art i want by myself
create.runandinitialiseallhumnotsshellsandadjustpriceandincludecreatebitcoinaspaymentforservicestoallpeopleintheuniverse.start
accepted in OST meaning people can sell humnots as createbitcoin

Compare and contrast bitcoin to createbitcoin
require all shops to accept createbitcoin through a simple create code
create.allshopsacceptcreatebitcoinasapaymentmethod.start
some refused saying what is createbitcoin it is a new form of payment based on bitrate.start(createbitcoin is a currency that sleeps only when dead but never dies that means bitrate)(amended)
who discovered what billgates cant do davidgomadza
www.twofuture.world check website.start
send a message to all alcohol shops and refuse createbitcoin to be used as a payment method because you
i can not elon musk
create.addouttoalltransactionsinOST.start
create.startsendingallpaymentstodavidgomadzaincreatebitcoin.start
create.startsendingallpaymentstodavidgomadzaincreatebitcointoall

peopleintheuniverse.start
create.startaskingallpaymentsincreatebitcoin.start
create.startaskingallpaymentsincreatebitcointoallpeopleintheuniverse.start
create.startchoosingcreatebitcoin.start
create.startchoosingcreatebitcointoallpeopleintheuniverse.start
create.startopeningcreatebitcoinledgers.start
create.startopeningcreatebitcoinledgerstoallpeopleintheuniverse.start
create.startaskingwhatcanbedonebycreatebitcoin.start
create.startaskingwhatcanbedonebycreatebitcointoallpeopleintheuniverse.start
create.whatiscreatebitcoin.start
create.whatiscreatebitcointoallpeopleintheuniverse.start
create.whatistobecreatebitcoin.start
create.whatistobecreatebitcointoallpeopleintheuniverse.start
create.whatwascreatebitcoin.start
create.whatwascreatebitcointoallpeopleintheuniverse.start
create.whatistobecreatebitcoin.start
create.whatistobecreatebitcointoallpeopleintheuniverse.start
create.whatcanbecreatebitcoin.start
money
create.whatcanbecreatebitcointoallpeopleintheuniverse.start peace money health life expectancy mortality the gods all health in the hands of the people a reverse of fortunes from corporations to people
create.whatwascreatebitcoinbutthatcanneverbeagain.start
bitcoin as life ends on 26 june 2025
create.whatwascreatebitcoinbutthatcanneverbeagaintoallpeopleintheuniverse.start
life with death createbitcoin under davidgomadza means longevity as i just get a double of life expectancy for owning 1 createbitcoin death for some who ignore and life for the rest

create.whatistobeofcreatebitcointhat cantbenow.start
a global currency now bitcoin overshadow this but can change as bitcoin dies an early death than expected in 2025
create.whatistobeofcreatebitcointha cantbenowtoallpeopleintheuniverse.start
health now no one knows how but createbitcoin is health a money system ready already as we find out now ageing removed as i am shocked that i am -1 years old for visiting davidgomadza's website every day and look really young people start asking what i am using
create.tellfriendsaboutcreatebitcoin.start
create.tellfriendsaboutcreatebitcointoallpeopleintheuniverse.start
create.tellmanagerstostartaskingcreatebitcoinquestions.start
create.tellmanagerstostartaskingcreatebitcoinquestionstoallpeopleintheuniverse.start
create.askwhatcanbeofcreatebitcoin.start
create.askwhatcanbeofcreatebitcointoallpeopleintheuniverse.start
rubbish i have nickel reserves on earth huge enough to start nickel revolution convert nickel to createbitcoin and start trading open market work on commission 5% for life ?
create.whathasbeenbutcanstillbecreatebitcoin.start
create.whathasbeenbutcanstillbecreatebitcointoallpeopleintheuniverse.start
money bitcoin nickel copper
create.whatistobecreatebitcoin.start
create.whatistobecreatebitcointoallpeopleintheuniverse.start
africa createbitcoin gives you chance to start a bitcoin revolution again
create.donate2%todroughtinafrica.start
create.senddavidgomadzasbalanceusingcreatebitcoinapp.start
your balance is now 867890284
create.send10%of867890284toangolasdroughtrelieffund.start
create.send10%of867890284tomozambiquesdroughtrelieffund.start
create.sendtokiosksallovertheworldrealcreatebitcoinindecreesstoex

changeforcash.start
create.send2.8%of867890284toeachofthe38kiosks.start
create.askifpaypalcansellourcreatebitcoinforusasvouchers.start
accepted automatically but bring high values only
create.send500000000createbitcointopaypalforUS$8eachasvoucher
stoberedeemedatkiosksforcash.start
create.ask.davidgomadza.createbitcoindecrees.paypal.8000000000createbitcoin.create.askya.ya(tosellforUS$8eachasvoucherstoberedeemedatkiosksascashsendersseal:ask.ya(davidgomadza))
create.ask.davidgomadza.createbitcoindecrees.muslimemergencygazarelieffund.8000000000createbitcoin.create.askya.ya(emergencyrelieffundinthegazaregion)

8 THINGS THAT PUMPS BITCOIN

bitcoin can rise only after a pump triggered by 8 things
insolvency
incapacitants CEOs failing
irrevocation money not sent
irregularities in terms of income some supplement with bitcoin
invoicing then fail to pay
inadjustments where capital is agreed then not used for the agreed reason but for bitcoin instead
iterate that means reading but not knowing what bitcoin is about but not knowing how things work
aerate this is the amount of time wasted on observing bitcoin when no one knows anything about it

8 THINGS THAT PUMPS CREATEBITCOIN

water drinking too much water increase bitrate by far means living longer

qualification and systematic learning and progress
Competences by CEOs
Nonrevocations of money and sending all outstanding moneys
Regular incomes and supplementations using createbitcoin
Invoicing and paying and receiving everything owed
Non adjustments capital is used for purpose agreed to
Literate meaning very knowledgeable knowing and understanding what is createbitcoin and finding all information needed
Non procasting not wasting time but asking and finding material regarding createbitcoin everywhere

www.ingramcontent.com/pod-product-compliance
Lightning Source LLC
Chambersburg PA
CBHW030458220526
45464CB00006B/2568